1936-1960

'I had just blown out the candles
on my ninth-birthday cake when, with
a second puff, I revealed to family
gathered around the table my secret
wish: "My name will be written in fiery
letters on the Champs-Élysées.¹"'

1936
Childhood in Oran

Yves Henri Donat Mathieu-Saint-Laurent was born 1 August, 1936 in Oran, Algeria, to Lucienne and Charles Mathieu-Saint-Laurent, an insurer and estate administrator. He had two sisters: Michèle, born in 1942, and Brigitte, born in 1945. In 1950, in Oran, the young boy was spellbound during a performance of Molière's *L'École des femmes* (*The School for Wives*), directed by Louis Jouvet, with costumes and sets by Christian Bérard. Yves Saint Laurent's passion for theatre never left him after that.

1953
Paper dolls

As a teenager, Yves Saint Laurent imagined the fashion house of his dreams, 'Yves Mathieu Saint Laurent Haute Couture Place-Vendôme'. From his mother's magazines, he cut out likeness of famous models of the time, like Bettina Ballard and Suzy Parker, and designed clothes and accessories made from cut-outs, gouache and ink for his 'paper dolls'. He went so far as to write up invitations and programmes for imaginary catwalk shows, which he slipped under the door to his sisters' room.

1953-1954
International Wool Secretariat Competition

In 1953, *Paris Match* announced the first annual fashion design competition organised by the International Wool Secretariat. Members of the jury included Christian Dior, Hubert de Givenchy and Jacques Fath. Yves Saint Laurent sent three sketches: a dress, a suit and a coat. He won third prize in the dress category. Through his father's connections, he met Michel de Brunhoff, director and editor-in-chief of *Vogue*. They began a long correspondence in the course of which de Brunhoff advised Yves Saint Laurent to complete his *baccalauréat* before considering any professional projects. In September 1954, with his diploma in hand, Yves Saint Laurent convinced his parents to let him move to Paris alone and enrol in the fashion school founded by the Chambre syndicale de la couture (Trade Association of High Fashion). Two years later, he took part in the competition once again and won first and third prizes in the dress category.

LEFT
Yves Saint Laurent with
his parents, Lucienne and
Charles, Oran, 1938.

ABOVE, LEFT
Yves Saint Laurent, Oran,
early 1940s.

ABOVE, RIGHT
Sketch for a costume (never
produced) for *La Reine Margot*
(*Queen Margot*) based
on the eponymous novel by
Alexandre Dumas, 1953.

OPPOSITE
Paper doll Bettina wearing
an evening gown,
between 1953 and 1955.

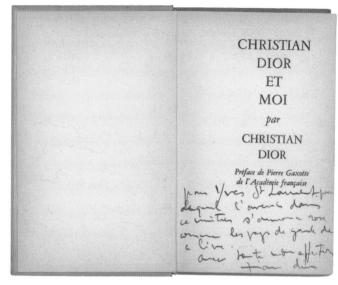

ABOVE
Dedication by Christian
Dior addressed to Yves Saint
Laurent on the title page of his
autobiography, *Christian Dior
et moi (Christian Dior and I)*,
1956: 'For Yves Saint Laurent,
whose future in this profession
promises to be as rosy as
the endpapers of this book.
Much love, Christian Dior.'

OPPOSITE
Christian Dior and Yves Saint
Laurent backstage at a fashion
show, 30 Avenue Montaigne,
Paris, 1955–1957.

ABOVE
Original storyboard from
La Vilaine Lulu, 1956.

1955

Early years at Dior

In the summer of 1955, Yves Saint Laurent sent fifty-some sketches to Michel de Brunhoff, who was struck by their similarity to Christian Dior's; he decided to show them to him. So Christian Dior met the young man and hired him on the spot to be his assistant. During this period, Yves Saint Laurent met Anne-Marie Muñoz, who became his closest collaborator, and Victoire Doutreleau, one of the most popular models of the time, whom he befriended.

1956

La Vilaine Lulu

The comic book *La Vilaine Lulu* (*Naughty Lulu*) recounts the trials of a cheeky, mischievous little girl inspired by a colleague at Dior who dressed up one evening during collection preparation. The cartoon, created in 1956 as an emotional release, was published in 1967 by Éditions Tchou, on Françoise Sagan's recommendation.

1957

The youngest fashion designer in the world

On 24 October, 1957, Christian Dior died suddenly from a heart attack in Italy. According to the designer's wishes, the young Yves Saint Laurent replaced him at the head of the most famous fashion house of the time. He was only 21 years old.

ABOVE
Preparatory sketch,
Yves Saint Laurent for
Christian Dior haute couture
collection, between 1958
and 1960.

1959
Cyrano de Bergerac

Yves Saint Laurent met dancer Zizi Jeanmaire and choreographer Roland Petit in 1956 during the 'Bal des têtes' thrown by Baron Alexis de Rédé at the Hôtel Lambert in Paris. They collaborated for the first time in 1959, on the ballet *Cyrano de Bergerac.* Yves Saint Laurent designed the costumes for the show, which was presented at the Alhambra.

1960
Final collection at Christian Dior

Yves Saint Laurent's sixth and final collection at Dior (Autumn/Winter 1960) was inspired by street fashion and the Beat Generation.

1958
'*Trapèze*' Collection

Yves Saint Laurent created his first collection (Spring/Summer 1958) for Dior, '*Trapèze*' (Trapeze), departing from Christian Dior's style by radically transforming the silhouette.

Meeting Pierre Bergé

Pierre Bergé was born on 14 November, 1930, on the Île d'Oléron. While in high school in La Rochelle, he developed a passion for literature. Without completing his *baccalauréat*, he headed to Paris and became a broker in the book industry. He was lucky enough to meet Jean Giono and Jean Cocteau, whom he befriended, as well as the painter Bernard Buffet, with whom he lived for eight years. Pierre Bergé and Yves Saint Laurent met during a dinner held at the Cloche d'or by Marie-Louise Bousquet, a representative for *Harper's Bazaar* in France, several days after the '*Trapèze*' collection was shown. They fell madly in love.

Jean Cocteau and Pierre Bergé, 1958.
Photograph by Édouard Dermit.

ABOVE, LEFT
Preparatory sketch for the
design *Bonne Conduite* (Good
Behaviour*). Spring/Summer
1958 Yves Saint Laurent for
Christian Dior's haute couture
collection *'Ligne Trapèze'*.
ABOVE, RIGHT
Sketch for the character
Roxane's costume in the ballet
Cyrano de Bergerac, 1959.
OPPOSITE
Sketch for the character
Cyrano's costume in the ballet
Cyrano de Bergerac, 1959.

Daytime ensemble *Zouzou*

Spring/Summer 1958 Yves Saint Laurent for
Christian Dior's haute couture collection, *'Ligne Trapèze'*.
Client design.
Grey wool (Maison Lesur) ensemble accessorised
with a small sprig of lily-of-the-valley.

Inv HC1958E178
Photograph by Laziz Hamani

Yves Saint Laurent 1936-1960

Composed of a dress and a jacket in Lesur grey wool flannel,
this was the last piece in the *'Trapèze'* collection show
presented on 30 January, 1958. In charge of Dior, Yves Saint
Laurent renewed the spirit of the suit with this piece: the
cut is sharp, the jacket and the dress form two overlapping
trapeziums, the austerity of flannel contrasts with the sprig
of lily-of-the-valley slipped in the pocket like a good-luck
charm. Already, the flat pleats of the skirt evoke the darted
trousers borrowed from mens' attire that would become
a foundation piece in the couturier's repertory. At the
time, it was common to give names to designs; this daytime
ensemble is called *Zouzou*, a nod to the little dog Yves Saint
Laurent left behind in Oran.

'After the ten-year reign of the cinched-waist New Look
launched in 1947 by Christian Dior, the *'Trapèze'* line frees
the waist and triumphs[2].'

'Yves Saint Laurent had incontestably the most novel
idea with the dress he baptised "shirt dress". Clinging at
the shoulders, it falls, supple, the body no longer appearing
boxed up but swaddled.[3]'

1958

Short daytime ensemble *Chicago*

Autumn/Winter 1960 Yves Saint Laurent
for Christian Dior haute couture collection.
Client design.
Patent crocodile-embossed leather jacket
with mink trim and skirt in black boucle wool.

Inv. HC1960H035
Photograph by Alexandre Guirkinger

The final Autumn/Winter 1960 collection created by
Yves Saint Laurent at Dior was called '*Suppleness, lightness,
life*'. Inspired by rebellious, beatnik street kids, this
predominately black collection was not as well-received as
preceding collections. This vest, inspired by biker jackets,
is dressed up with crocodile-embossed leather trimmed
in mink and accompanied by a fur cap. In bringing 'rocker
jackets' into Dior's hushed rooms, he provoked
an unprecedented rupture.

'My last collection for Dior deeply shocked the fashion
world. [...] All this inspiration taken from the street
was considered very vulgar by many people perched on
golden chairs at catwalk shows. Yet, it was the first major
manifestation of my style. [...] Social structures were
starting to break down. The street was a new source
of pride, its own style, and was a source of inspiration
for me, as it would often be thereafter.[4]'

1961-1970

'The most beautiful clothes that can dress a woman are the arms of the man she loves. But for those who haven't had the fortune of finding this happiness, I am there.[5]'

LEFT Maurice Hogenboom, *Yves Saint Laurent,* Paris, 1964.

1963
Cinema and music hall

Yves Saint Laurent designed Claudia Cardinale's costumes for Blake Edwards' *The Pink Panther*, as well as Zizi Jeanmaire's music hall outfits for the revue choreographed by Roland Petit including the routine *Champagne rosé* (Pink Champagne).

1964
First *Y* fragrance

In 1964, Yves Saint Laurent launched his first fragrance for women, *Y*.

1961
Creation of the fashion house

After several deferments, Yves Saint Laurent was drafted on 2 September, 1960 to serve in the armed forces during the Algerian war. Marc Bohan replaced him at Dior. Upon his discharge, he fell into depression and was transferred to the military hospital at Val-de-Grâce. There, he decided to start his own fashion house with Pierre Bergé. After securing the necessary funding from J. Mack Robinson, an American industrialist from Atlanta, the fashion house was officially created on 4 December, 1961. Several colleagues at Dior took their chances and followed him.

1962
First collection under the name Yves Saint Laurent

In the plainly decorated rooms at 30 bis rue Spontini, the 101 designs in the first collection (Spring/Summer 1962) were extremely well received.

ABOVE
Yves Saint Laurent,
11 Rue Jean-Goujon, Paris,
December 1961.

ABOVE, LEFT
Presentation of Yves Saint
Laurent's first haute couture
collection, 30 bis Rue Spontini,
Paris, 29 January 1962.

ABOVE, RIGHT, TOP
Original sketch for an
afternoon dress.
Spring/Summer 1962
haute couture collection.

ABOVE, RIGHT, BOTTOM
Sketch for Zizi Jeanmaire's
costume in the dance
routine *Champagne rosé*
(Pink Champagne) in the
music hall review *Spectacle
Zizi Jeanmaire*, 1963.

OPPOSITE
Preparatory sketch for the
Y fragrance bottle, 1964.

1965
Dresses in homage to Piet Mondrian

Yves Saint Laurent designed the *Mondrian* and *Poliakoff* dresses for the Autumn/Winter 1965 collection.

Shows

In 1965, Yves Saint Laurent met the dancer Rudolf Noureev. The couturier created the costumes for the ballet *Notre-Dame de Paris*, using silhouettes from the '*Mondrian*' collection for certain designs.

ABOVE, LEFT
Atelier specification sheet, known as a 'Bible', for a cocktail dress. Homage to Piet Mondrian. Autumn/Winter 1965 haute couture collection.
ABOVE, RIGHT
Gérard Pataa, *Cocktail dress worn by Léo*. Homage to Piet Mondrian. Autumn/Winter 1965 haute couture collection. 30 bis Rue Spontini, Paris, July 1965.
OPPOSITE
Sketch for Phœbus' costume in the ballet *Notre-Dame de Paris*, 1965.

1966
First tuxedo

Yves Saint Laurent created one of
his iconic pieces, the tuxedo, for the
Autumn/Winter 1966 collection.

ABOVE, LEFT
Atelier specification sheet
known as a 'Bible' for the first
tuxedo. Autumn/Winter 1966
haute couture collection.

ABOVE, RIGHT
Original sketch for the first
tuxedo. Autumn/Winter 1966
haute couture collection.

OPPOSITE
Gérard Pataa, *First tuxedo worn
by Ulla*. Autumn/Winter 1966
haute couture collection.

1966

SAINT LAURENT
rive gauche

On 26 September, 1966, Yves Saint Laurent opened his first ready-to-wear boutique, SAINT LAURENT *rive gauche*, at 21 rue de Tournon in Paris. Catherine Deneuve is the honorary patron. This new line gave even more women the opportunity to wear Saint Laurent and to adopt a modern style perfectly in step with their era. Yves Saint Laurent asserted a 'certain way of life, more than a certain way of dressing[6]' and stated loud and clear, 'Down with the Ritz, long live the street.[7]'

This first boutique paved the way for what fashion has become. The approach was novel, as much in how designs were created as in how they were produced and distributed.

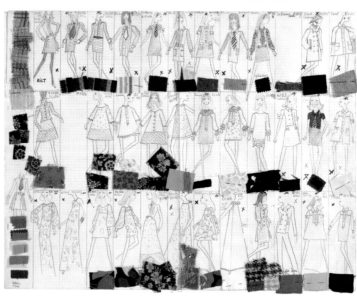

1969

marraKech le 8 Décembre

Ma chère Zizi
mon cher Roland
Je pense à vous beaucoup
Je vous embrasse très très
tendrement ainsi que
Valentine. A Bientôt
Yves
Pierre vous embrasse très fort aussi.

Discovering Morocco

In September 1966, Yves Saint Laurent and Pierre Bergé discovered Marrakech. They fell in love with the city and immediately decided to buy the Dar el-Hanch home, the 'serpent house' located in the medina. This encounter with Morocco marked the appearance of colour in the couturier's creations. He got into the habit of traveling there at the beginning of nearly every December and June to design his collections.

PAGE LEFT, TOP
Meerson, *Advert for the opening of the SAINT LAURENT* rive gauche *ready-to-wear boutique*, 1966.
PAGE LEFT, BOTTOM
Collection board.
Spring/Summer 1967
SAINT LAURENT
rive gauche collection.
ABOVE, LEFT
Letter from Yves Saint Laurent to Zizi Jeanmaire and Roland Petit, 1969.

ABOVE, RIGHT
Yves Saint Laurent in Morocco in the 1960s. Photograph by Pierre Bergé.
OPPOSITE
Yves Saint Laurent on a bike in Morocco in the 1960s. Photograph by Pierre Bergé.

1967
Dresses in homage to Bambara art

Alongside his first tennis-striped trouser suit, Yves Saint Laurent created a series of dresses inspired by African Bambara art for the Spring/Summer 1967 collection.

Meeting Betty Catroux

Yves Saint Laurent met model Betty Catroux at a party at the famous club *Chez Régine*. A true creature of the night, unconventional and slender, she was like a twin sister to him. 'We were both flaxen-haired,' says Betty Catroux, 'long hair, skinny, dressed alike in black leather. [...] He's been my best friend ever since. We have the same tendencies, we're insanely comfortable together, as if we were the same flesh and blood.[8]'

Catherine Deneuve

The year 1967 marked the beginning of a long collaboration between the couturier and actress Catherine Deneuve. He designed her costumes for Luis Buñuel's film *Belle de jour*. In 1968, he dressed her in Alain Cavalier's *La Chamade* (*Heartbeat*), and in 1969 in François Truffaut's *La Sirène du Mississippi* (*Mississippi Mermaid*).

PAGE LEFT, LEFT
Original sketch for an evening
ensemble. Homage to Bambara
art. Spring/Summer 1967
haute couture collection.

PAGE LEFT, RIGHT
Jean-Paul Cadé, *Evening
ensemble worn by Danielle Luquet
de Saint Germain. Homage to
Bambara art. Spring/Summer
1967 haute couture collection.*
Jardin des serres d'Auteuil
(Auteuil Greenhouses),
Bois de Boulogne, Paris.

ABOVE, TOP
Yves Saint Laurent and Betty
Catroux in the 1980s.

ABOVE, LEFT
Yves Saint Laurent and
Catherine Deneuve wearing
tuxedos for the 20th
anniversary of the fashion
house celebrated at the Lido,
Paris, 29 January 1982.

ABOVE, RIGHT
Catherine Deneuve's daytime
dress worn for the role of
Séverine Serizy in the film
Belle de jour, 1967.

OPPOSITE
Sketch for Catherine
Deneuve's costume for the role
of Séverine Serizy in the film
Belle de jour, 1967.

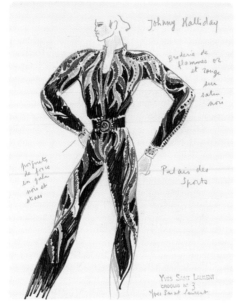

Loulou de La Falaise
and Fernando Sanchez,
Marrakech,1970s.
ABOVE
Sketch for Johnny Hallyday's
costume for his concert at the
Palais des Sports, Paris, 1971.
OPPOSITE
Sketch for Zizi Jeanmaire's
costume in the dance routine
Ouverture in the music hall
show *La Revue*, 1970.

LOVE

Each year, except for 1978 and 1993, Yves Saint Laurent designed a greeting card in the form of a poster, which he sent to friends, clients, suppliers and collaborators. A combination of drawing and collage, the card, which every year featured the word 'LOVE' like a leitmotif, became a house ritual.

1969
Meeting Loulou de La Falaise

Loulou de La Falaise met Yves Saint Laurent and Pierre Bergé in 1969 through designer and mutual friend, Fernando Sanchez. Her free-flowing style, her love of clothes gleaned from flea markets and her gift for putting jewellery together immediately charmed the couturier. She joined the studio in 1972 and oversaw accessories, knits and fabrics for 30 years.

1970
Shows

The year 1970 witnessed a number of collaborations with the entertainment industry. The couturier designed the costumes for the 37 routines in *La Revue* for Zizi Jeanmaire. He also created the costumes for Sylvie Vartan at the Olympia and, the following year, for her then-husband Johnny Halliday, for a concert at the *Palais des Sports*.

Rue de Babylone

In 1970, Yves Saint Laurent and Pierre Bergé moved to 55 rue de Babylone in Paris. The duplex became the backdrop for their art and furniture collections.

ABOVE
Greeting card 'LOVE', 1972.
BELOW
Vladimir Sichov, *Yves Saint Laurent and Pierre Bergé in their apartment*, 55 Rue de Babylone, Paris, 1982.

Boating ensemble, first peacoat

Spring/Summer 1962 haute couture collection.
Prototype. Atelier Georges.
Peacoat in navy blue wool (Maison Prud'homme),
shantung blouse and trousers (Maison Pétillaud).

Inv. HC1962E082
Photograph by Sophie Carre

The peacoat made a noteworthy appearance when it
opened the Spring/Summer 1962 catwalk show.
The couturier drew on the functionality of the sailor's work
garment, which he feminised by adding gold buttons and
pairing it with elegant white trousers and plaited leather
mules. Reinterpreting a utilitarian garment, he urbanised it,
announcing the first inklings of the navy look he returned
to in the Spring/Summer 1966 collection, which included
striped jerseys and sailor caps.

    The peacoat emerged as a manifesto of what was to
become the 'Saint Laurent' style, alongside the trouser suit,
tuxedo, jumpsuit and trench coat, garments borrowed
from men to create the modern woman's wardrobe.

1962

Cocktail dress,
Homage to Piet Mondrian

Autumn/Winter 1965 haute couture collection.
Prototype. Atelier Blanche.
Dress in *Paris Midi* and *Air France* wool jersey blocks
(Maison Racine).

Inv. HC1965H081
Photograph by Alexandre Guirkinger

While thumbing through a book about the painter
Piet Mondrian given to him by his mother, the young
couturier caught a glimpse of his future collection. 'I suddenly
realised that dresses should no longer be composed of lines,
but of colours. I realised that we had to stop thinking of
garments as sculpture and that we had to, on the contrary,
think of them as bodies in motion.[9]'

Yves Saint Laurent appropriated the abstract painter's
work by transforming a painting into a three-dimensional
garment. With this short, straight dress, replete with lines
and solid colours from neck to hem, Yves Saint Laurent
paid homage to a painter he admired. Not content to make
a simple allusion, he gave him life and movement.
'Mondrian is purity and one can go no further in purity in
painting. This is a purity that joins with that of the Bauhaus.
The masterpiece of the twentieth century is a Mondrian.[10]'

In the same collection, Yves Saint Laurent created dresses
in homage to the painter Serge Poliakoff and ended his
catwalk show with a wedding gown in wool jersey and ivory
silk ribbon. The dress is like a cocoon that embraces the body;
it alludes to Russian dolls, the *matriochkas*.

1965

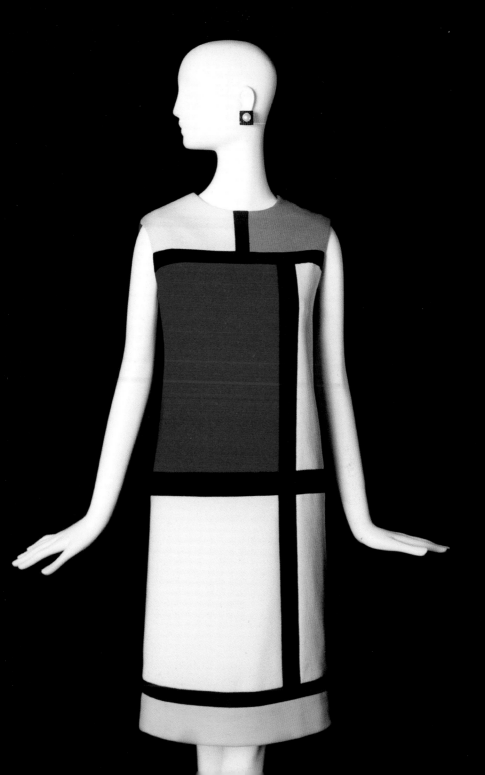

First tuxedo

Autumn/Winter 1966 haute couture collection.
Prototype. Atelier Mario.
Jacket and trousers in *grain de poudre* wool and silk satin
(Maison Dormeuil), and cotton batiste blouse.
Inv. HC1966H076
Photograph by Alexandre Guirkinger

To smoke their cigars after dinner, men in 1880s England donned
a special jacket, the 'smoking jacket', equipped with wide satin
lapels onto which ashes slid without leaving a trace. Presented by
Yves Saint Laurent for the Autumn/Winter 1966 haute couture
collection, the tuxedo was not the success it was expected to be
in the eyes of the haute couture clientele. Several months later,
its ready-to-wear version was met with enthusiasm.

Yves Saint Laurent feminised the tuxedo with a long jacket,
a white organza blouse topped with a jabot, an ascot tie, a silk
satin belt and heeled ankle boots. It became the preserve of
emancipated women, claiming the right to wear evening trousers
like men, transgressing traditional conventions and flouting
the rules of seduction. The couturier reinvented this piece
throughout his career.

'The greatest change was the discovery of my own style,
without the influence of others. It was the tuxedo and the sheer
blouse. There I started a conversation with women and began
to understand what it is to be a modern woman.'

In the same collection, alongside the tuxedo, a symbol of
simplicity, Yves Saint Laurent presented brightly coloured
dresses with simple motifs in homage to Pop art. The following
year, for the Spring/Summer 1967 collection, the couturier
designed his first trouser suit.

Prototype.
Organza silk dress embroidered with Rhodoïd,
wooden beads and seed beads (Maison Lanel).

Inv. HC1967E108
Photograph by Alexandre Guirkinger

In January 1967, the couturier presented a Spring/Summer
collection inspired by African culture. While dress lengths –
very long or very short – call to mind Western womenswear
classics, the embroidery in non-precious materials like
wood, raphia and Rhodoïd evoke traditional costumes
from Sub-Saharan Africa, flouting haute couture cliches.
The designs also allude to African art, specifically West
African Bambara statuary. Literal references are absent
from this collection; Yves Saint Laurent drew freely upon
culture to create a very personal vision.

    In March 1967, *Harper's Bazaar* described the collection
as 'a fantasy of primitive genius shells and jungle jewel[le]ry
clustered to cover the bosom and hips, latticed to bare
the midriff.[12]'

FOLLOWING SPREAD, LEFT Original sketch for the evening gown known as *Bambara*.
Spring/Summer 1967 haute couture collection.
FOLLOWING SPREAD, RIGHT Detail from the evening gown known as *Bambara*.
Spring/Summer 1967 haute couture collection.

1152
Esther
sur
lizzie

broderie
toute noire

108

119

1971-1980

'Fashion changes, but style endures.[13]'

1971
The Forties Collection

Inspired by Paloma Picasso, who built her style around garments gleaned from the flea markets,
Yves Saint Laurent designed a collection (Spring/Summer 1971) alluding to Occupied Paris; its audacity was cause for scandal.

Pour homme

To draw attention to the launch of the fragrance *Pour homme*, his first eau de toilette for men, Yves Saint Laurent chose to pose nude for photographer Jeanloup Sieff. The image provoked a stream of commentary of all stripes. 'It was in 1971,' recalls the photographer, 'we were young, beautiful and intelligent! Yves Saint Laurent launched his first eau de toilette and he wanted to pose nude for the advert because he wanted to "shock"[14].'

ABOVE
Atelier specification sheet known as a 'Bible' for a formal dress. Spring/Summer 1971 haute couture collection.
OPPOSITE
Coat embroidered with mouths. Spring/Summer 1971 haute couture collection. Photograph by Sophie Carre.

1972

Zizi je t'aime !

In 1972, the couturier designed the costumes for the revue *Zizi, je t'aime!* at the Casino de Paris. When Edmonde Charles-Roux asked him what he gained from the music hall, Yves Saint Laurent replied, 'Speed. It's all there in the music hall. To create a world: three accessories. [...] Having a sense of the grand and of the postage-stamp scale at the same time. And the music hall, more so than the theatre, is life turned upside down. Poor materials look rich and vice versa. Forget the normal... Not easy.[15]'

Andy Warhol

The painter Andy Warhol, whom Yves Saint Laurent met in 1966, carried out several portraits of the couturier based on Polaroid photographs.

1974

5, avenue Marceau

The fashion house moved to 5 avenue Marceau, to a Second Empire *hôtel particulier* and in doing so, drew closer to haute couture territory.

ABOVE, TOP
Sketch for a dancer's costume in the dance routine *Night and Day* for the music hall show *Zizi je t'aime!*, 1972.
ABOVE
Portrait of Yves Saint Laurent by Andy Warhol, 1972.
OPPOSITE
Claus Ohm, *The fashion house façade*, 5 Avenue Marceau, Paris, 1976.

OPPOSITE, TOP
Evening ensemble worn by
Laure Daqualord. Autumn/
Winter 1976 haute couture
collection known as '*Opéra-
Ballets russes*'. Inter-Continental
Hotel, Paris, July 1976.

OPPOSITE
Developmental drawing for
two evening ensembles.
Autumn/Winter 1976
haute couture collection
known as '*Opéra-Ballets russes*'.

BELOW
Evening ensemble of Chinese
inspiration worn by Marie
Helvin. Autumn/Winter
1977 haute couture collection
known as '*Chinoise et opium*'.
Inter-Continental Hotel,
Paris, July 1977.

1976
'Opéra-Ballets russes'
Collection

For the first time, Yves Saint Laurent presented his collection outside of his own premises at the Inter-Continental Hotel, rue de Castiglione. The Autumn/Winter 1976 'Opéra-Ballets russes' (Opera-Russian Ballets) collection drew inspiration from Tsarist Russia and Diaghilev's ballets, while accentuating the theatricality and opulence of ornamentation.

1977
'Chinoise et Opium'
Collection

Yves Saint Laurent designed a collection (Autumn/Winter 1977) inspired by China, without ever having travelled there. It is one of his most beautiful imaginary journeys.

Opium

In July 1977, as the Autumn/Winter collection 'Chinoise et Opium' (Chinese and Opium) was being presented, the fragrance was launched in France with the tagline 'Opium: for women addicted to Yves Saint Laurent.' Yves Saint Laurent designed the bottle, the press kit, the launch party and the advertising campaign coordinated by Maïmé Arnodin and Denise Fayolle's Mafia agency. Helmut Newton created the image, with Jerry Hall as the muse. For the fragrance's release in 1978 in the United States, a party was hosted in New York for 1000 guests on the tall ship *Peking*. 'I didn't want any other name for this fragrance... It's a fragrance that evokes everything I love, Eastern refinement, Imperial China, exoticism.[16]'

ABOVE
Preparatory sketch for the *Opium* fragrance bottle, 1977.
BELOW
Preparatory sketch for the fragrance *Opium*, 1978.

1978
Cosmetics

In 1978, Yves Saint Laurent launched his first cosmetics line, declaring, 'The woman I dress needs a face.'

L'Aigle à deux têtes (The Eagle with Two Heads)

The couturier designed costumes and sets for Jean Cocteau's *The Eagle with Two Heads*, for the Athénée Louis Jouvet theatre, acquired by Pierre Bergé the previous year. The project took up a childhood project Yves Saint Laurent had abandoned on the drawing board after his father brought back photos from Jean Cocteau's film from Paris.

1979
Homage to Pablo Picasso and Serge de Diaghilev

For this collection (Autumn/Winter 1979), Yves Saint Laurent drew on the work of Pablo Picasso by reinterpreting the harlequin figure as well as the artist's famous cubist lines.

1980
Majorelle Garden

Yves Saint Laurent and Pierre Bergé discovered the Majorelle Garden in 1966, during their first stay in Marrakech. They acquired it in 1980 to save it from being turned into a real estate venture. They decide to live in the artist's villa, renamed Villa Oasis, and restore the garden to 'make Majorelle Garden the most beautiful garden – the one Jacques Majorelle designed and imagined.'

BELOW, LEFT
Atelier specification sheet known as a 'Bible' for a 'Picasso-suit'. Homage to Pablo Picasso. Autumn/Winter 1979 haute couture collection.

BELOW, RIGHT
Original sketch for the *Robe au visage (Dress with a face)*. Homage to Pablo Picasso. Autumn/Winter 1979 haute couture collection.

ABOVE, LEFT
Preparatory sketch
for *L'Aigle à deux têtes*
(The Eagle with Two Heads)
coat of arms, 1978.

ABOVE, RIGHT
Edwige Feuillère and Martine
Chevallier playing the queen
and Édith de Berg in act one of
L'Aigle à deux têtes, 1978.

OPPOSITE
Costume sketches for the
Queen and Count Foëhn in act
one of *L'Aigle à deux têtes*, 1978.

BELOW
Jacques Majorelle's former
studio preserved by the
Bergé-Saint Laurent couple,
Marrakech. Photograph by
Nicolas Mathéus.

Evening coat

Spring/Summer 1971 haute couture collection.
Prototype. Atelier Jean-Pierre.
Green fox coat.

Inv. HC1971E090
Photograph by Alexandre Guirkinger

The Spring/Summer 1971 collection known as '*Forties*'
or '*Liberation*' marked the end of the 1960s Futurist years
and paved the way for a 1970s retro spirit tinged with
scandal. Square shoulders, puffed sleeves, wedge heels,
short dresses cut on the bias with plunging necklines,
and provocative cosmetics made aesthetic references to
Occupied Paris. Faced with criticism of a rare vehemence,
Yves Saint Laurent declared, 'I prefer to be shocking than
to get bored doing the same old thing.[17]' But retro style
quickly took over the street, inspiring many designers.
New York soon declared, 'Old is in![18]'

   With this fox coat dyed an unnatural green and worn
close to the skin over a black silk jersey bodysuit and
accessorised with slingback heels, Yves Saint Laurent
created a smouldering silhouette that broke with
every bourgeois convention.

1971

Evening gown created for Jane Birkin the Proust ball, 1971

Silk crepe and floral guipure lace gown,
with silk satin waistband.

Inv. 2013.06.01
Photograph by Sophie Carre

Marcel Proust's *À la recherche du temps perdu* (*In Search of Lost Time*) had a profound impact on Yves Saint Laurent. 'Proust is the one who said the most about women, and whose life is a little similar to mine.[19]' Like Marcel Proust, the couturier admitted to being born with nervous depression and belonging to the same 'magnificent and pitiful family (of neurotics) that is the salt of the earth.[20]'

On 2 December, 1971, Marie-Hélène de Rothschild hosted a costume ball at her Château de Ferrières to celebrate the 100th anniversary of the birth of Marcel Proust. For the occasion, Yves Saint Laurent designed dresses for Nan Kempner, Hélène Rochas, Jane Birkin and Marie-Hélène de Rothschild.

Jane Birkin's dress draws on the Belle Epoque spirit of the 1900s, with a flowing silhouette and billowing folds, and lace worthy of Countess Greffulhe. Yves Saint Laurent recreated a Proustian spirit and transported the guests into the world of his favourite writer.

1971

Evening ensemble

Autumn/Winter 1976 haute couture collection known as *'Opéra-Ballets russes'*.
Prototype. Atelier Esther.
Silk velvet waistcoat (Maison Léonard) fastened by lace frogging
(Maison Denez).
Printed silk chiffon blouse with metal embroidery (Maison Abraham).
Silk gazar skirt and silk velvet yoke (Maison Léonard).
Inv. HC1976H040.
Photograph by Sophie Carre

The wealth of fabrics, colours and ornamentation in this collection
evoked the couturier's vision of Russia, where traditional peasant
garb mingled with that of the Tzars, as well as Léon Bakst's costumes
for Serge de Diaghilev's ballets.

Here, the couturier revived the idea of luxury in fashion;
his cashmere shawls, shot silk skirts, sheer blouses topped with
tatting-bedecked waistcoats were immensely success.

'It's a painterly collection inspired by Delacroix's *Odalisques*,
Ingrès' women, Van Eyck's *Woman with a Pearl Earring*,
[in fact, Vermeer's *Girl with a Pearl Earring*], La Tour, Rembrandt,
Degas' dancers, with their black corselet, but also by
Visconti's *Senso*, the Civil War, Marlène de Sternberg.
It's extremely selfish, because I exhibited, much more than dresses,
all the painting I love.[21]'

FOLLOWING SPREAD, LEFT Detail from an evening ensemble. Autumn/Winter 1976
haute couture collection known as *'Opéra-Ballets russes'*. Photograph by Sophie Carre.
FOLLOWING SPREAD, RIGHT Developmental drawing for an evening ensemble.
Autumn/Winter 1976 haute couture collection known as *'Opéra-Ballets russes'*.

Evening ensemble of Chinese inspiration

Autumn/Winter 1976 haute couture collection.
Prototype. Ateliers Jean-Pierre and Catherine.
Damask silk jacket in a scroll pattern, silk crepe blouse
(Maison Abraham) and silk velvet trousers.
Inv. HC1977H094
Photograph by Sophie Carre

'I've finally cracked the secret of the Imperial City where
I liberate you, my aesthetic ghosts, my queens, my divas,
my whirlwind parties, my inky, crêpe de Chine nights,
my Coromandel lacquer, my artificial lakes, and
my hanging gardens.[22]'

The Autumn/Winter 1977 collection titled '*Chinoise
et Opium*', an homage to the China of the couturier's
imagination, included among other things, capes, waxed
jackets, silk damask, embroidered velvet, imperial dresses
and taffeta trousers. The looks were accessorised with
mink-trimmed suede ankle boots, conical hats and jewellery
bearing motifs from Imperial China.

1977

1981-1989

'Clothing is above all a way of life.
It teaches you to live happily. It can
liberate you, help you find yourself,
do what will make you a limitless being.
Isn't elegance forgetting what one
is wearing?[23]'

LEFT Yves Saint Laurent at his desk, studio at 5 Avenue Marceau, Paris, 1986.

1981

Dresses inspired by Henri Matisse and Fernand Léger

For the Autumn/Winter 1981 collection, Yves Saint Laurent found inspiration in two of his favourite artists: he borrowed Fauvist colours and motifs from Henri Matisse, and Cubist, even Tubist, lines from Fernand Léger.

Marguerite Yourcenar

Poet and novelist Marguerite Yourcenar was elected to Roger Caillois' seat in the Académie française on 6 March, 1980. The first woman to walk the Académie's halls on 22 January, 1981, she wore an *académicienne's* robe designed by Yves Saint Laurent. As her installation ceremony approached, she said, 'I've always been hostile to uniforms, so I'll wear the simplest possible dress, but one I hope is pretty...[24]'

1982

20th anniversary of the fashion house

Yves Saint Laurent decided to celebrate the fashion house's 20th anniversary at the famous Lido Cabaret. The entire staff was invited to a gala dinner at which the couturier received The International Fashion Award from the Council of Fashion Designers of America from Diana Vreeland herself, the famous editor-in-chief of *Vogue* magazine.

Kouros

Yves Saint Laurent released a masculine fragrance under the name *Kouros*, inspired by Ancient Greek statues of young men. The couturier himself designed the press release using collages in concordant blue and silver.

ABOVE
Original sketch for an evening gown inspired by Henri Matisse. Autumn/Winter 1981 haute couture collection.

ABOVE, LEFT
Evening ensemble inspired
by Henri Matisse worn
by Edia Vairelli.
Autumn/Winter 1981
haute couture collection.
Inter-Continental Hotel,
Paris, July 1981.

ABOVE, RIGHT
Sketch for an
académicienne's robe
for Marguerite
Yourcenar, 1981.
OPPOSITE
Preparatory collage for
the fragrance *Kouros*, 1981.

AA AA A AA. AHHH... PARIS

HOMMAGE À CHAVAL

ABOVE
Excerpt from the press release
developed by Jean-Paul Goude
for the 15th anniversary
of the fragrance *Paris*.

OPPOSITE
Yves Saint Laurent surrounded
by his models after the
Autumn/Winter 1983 catwalk
show during which the
fragrance *Paris* was presented.
Inter-Continental Hotel,
Paris, July 1983.

1983
Paris

In 1983, *Paris*, a fragrance for women, is released in a faceted spherical bottle. 'Paris, prestigious, dazzling. Your blazing, crackling fireworks make the world sparkle. For this new fragrance, I choose your name because there's none more beautiful. Because I love you, My Paris.²⁵'
Advertising executive Jean-Paul Goude organised a spectacular campaign on the fragrance's 15th anniversary.

Metropolitan Museum of Art

In 1983, the Costume Institute of the Metropolitan Museum of Art of New York, under the supervision of Diana Vreeland, organised the first retrospective exhibition for a living couturier: 'Yves Saint Laurent – 25 Years of Design'. It is a great success for the American museum, which receives more than 1 million visitors. The exhibition then travelled around the world, first to Beijing's Palace of Fine Arts in 1985, then to the Musée des Arts de la Mode in Paris in 1986, then the Tretyakov Gallery in Moscow and the Hermitage Museum in Leningrad (Saint Petersburg) in 1987, and the Sezon Museum of Art in Tokyo in 1990.

Château Gabriel

In January 1983, Yves Saint Laurent and Pierre Bergé purchased Château Gabriel in Benerville-sur-Mer, in Normandy, where Marcel Proust met book publisher Gaston Gallimard. Jacques Grange was charged with creating a Belle Epoque interior design in homage to the writer. Each room was named after a character from *In Search of Lost Time*; and so Yves Saint Laurent became Charles Swann and Pierre Bergé Baron Charlus.

1988
'*Cubist*' Collection

Yves Saint Laurent paid homage to Georges Braque, Juan Gris and Vincent Van Gogh in this Spring/Summer 1988 collection.

Fête de L'Humanité

On 9 September, 1988, Yves Saint Laurent created a buzz when he presented 180 designs at the *Fête de L'Humanité*. In the presence of 50,000 visitors and Communist Party activists, he reinvented the catwalk show by democratising access through a mainstream event.

1989
Bougainvillea

Amid the trouser-suits, tuxedos and striped shirts, Yves Saint Laurent peppered his Spring/Summer 1989 catwalk show with a series of colourful capes in bougainvillea patterns inspired by Moroccan gardens.

ABOVE, TOP
Evening ensemble. Homage to Georges Braque. Spring/Summer 1988 haute couture collection.
Photograph by Sophie Carre.

ABOVE, CENTRE
Evening ensemble worn by Amalia Vairelli. Homage to Pablo Picasso. Spring/Summer 1988 haute couture collection. 5 Avenue Marceau, Paris, January 1988.
Polaroid by house staff.

OPPOSITE
Fashion show for the Fête de L'Humanité, La Courneuve, 9 September 1988.

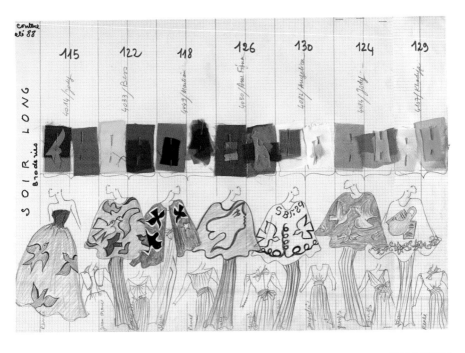

ABOVE
Collection board for
'Long Evening/Embroidery'.
Spring/Summer 1988
haute couture collection.

OPPOSITE
Evening ensemble known
as 'Bougainvillea' worn
by Diana Bienvenu.
Spring/Summer 1989
haute couture collection.
Inter-Continental Hotel,
Paris, January 1989.

Long evening gown
inspired by Henri Matisse

Autumn/Winter 1981 haute couture collection.
Prototype. Atelier Esther.
Gown in satin gazar and silk satin (Maison Taroni) with silk
satin appliqué-patchwork (Maisons Gandini and Perceval)
and embroidered silk taffeta (Maison Brossin de Méré).
Inv. HC1981H143
Photograph by Sophie Carre

Throughout his career, Yves Saint Laurent maintained
a dialog with art by referencing and reinterpreting great
painters: in 1965 with Piet Mondrian, in 1966 with Tom
Wesselmann, and again in 1988 with Georges Braque.
For the Autumn/Winter 1981 collection, the couturier drew
inspiration from the painter Henri Matisse, as illustrated
in this evening gown in shimmering colours and motifs from
The Red Room, painted in 1908. 'My aim was not to compare
myself to the masters, but to, at the most, connect with
them and learn from their genius.[26]'

Daytime ensemble

Autumn/Winter 1986 haute couture collection.
Prototype. Atelier Alain.
Trench and silk ensemble in panther-print silk satin
(Maison Abraham).

Inv. HC1986H037
Photograph by Sophie Carre

The trench coat is one of Yves Saint Laurent's iconic
designs; it first appeared in the 1962 Autumn/Winter 1962
collection. The couturier unrelentingly reinterpreted this
contemporary wardrobe classic, whose roots stretch back
to English officers who used it to shield themselves from
bad weather.

The Autumn/Winter 1986 trench, with leopard print
created by Maison Abraham, is a wonderful example of
variation on a classic. Long reserved for pin-ups, this motif
became all the rage in France thanks to Christian Dior's
reinterpretation in the 1950s. Following in his master's
footsteps, Yves Saint Laurent continually reinvented
the motif, making it timeless and ensuring it would never
go out of style.

Short evening jackets known as 'Irises' and 'Sunflowers'.
Homage to Vincent Van Gogh

Spring/Summer 1988 haute couture collection.
Prototypes. Atelier Jean-Pierre.
Silk organza jackets embroidered with sequins, ribbons,
tube-shaped pearls and seed beads (Maison Lesage).

Inv. HC1988E093 et HC1988E094
Photograph by Alexandre Guirkinger

For the Spring/Summer 1988 collection, the couturier
created two embroidered jackets in homage to Van Gogh's
Sunflowers and *Irises*. They are said to be the most expensive
pieces in the history of haute couture because each required
600 hours of work, carried out by Maison Lesage.
Pearls, sequins and ribbons lend texture and movement,
transfiguring the painter's style. Rhinestone buttons by
Maison Desrues accentuate the precious nature of the two
pieces. Despite its impressive price tag, the jacket in homage
to *Irises* was ordered in a longer version to make a coat.

FOLLOWING SPREAD, LEFT Detail from short jacket known as 'Irises'.
Homage to Vincent Van Gogh. Spring/Summer 1988 haute couture collection.
Photograph by Sophie Carre.
FOLLOWING SPREAD, RIGHT Evening ensemble worn by Jody. Homage to Vincent
Van Gogh. Spring/Summer 1988 haute couture collection. 5 Avenue Marceau,
Paris, January 1988. Polaroid by house staff.

1988

93.
BESS 93 4034
P.E.88

Silk gazar cape embroidered with organza silk bougainvillea flowers and seed beads (Maison Lemarié). Dress and belt in silk muslin (Maison Bianchini and Maison Saris).

Inv. HC1989E071
Photograph by Sophie Carre

The bougainvillea capes from the Spring/Summer 1989 collection are a nod to luxurious Moroccan gardens. Yves Saint Laurent developed his taste for colour in Morocco. He dared to make bold colour pairings: fuchsia pink and orange, emerald green and lagoon blue, bright red and deep violet. The colours blend and clash, never detracting from one another. Like personal "ready-to-wear gardens", the capes exist in an embroidered version, as well as in superb print motifs.

'We've lived in Marrakech for 40 years. Yves Saint Laurent and I are indebted viscerally and artistically to Morocco, our adopted country,[27]' shares Pierre Bergé.

FOLLOWING SPREAD, LEFT Detail from long evening ensemble known as 'Bougainvillea'. Spring/Summer 1989 haute couture collection. Photograph by Sophie Carre.
FOLLOWING SPREAD, RIGHT Preparatory sketch for evening ensemble known as 'Bougainvillaea' (détail). Spring/Summer 1989 haute couture collection.

1990-2008

'I'm aware of having executed my work with precision and exigence for many long years. Without concession. What has always come first to me is respect for a métier that is not quite an art, but which needs an artist in order to exist. I think I have been true to the teenager who showed his first sketches to Christian Dior with unwavering faith and conviction. That faith and conviction have never left me. I fought for elegance and beauty.[28]'

LEFT André Rau, *Yves Saint Laurent*, 5 Avenue Marceau, Paris, 1992.

1990
'Hommages' (*Homages*)
Collection

With the Spring/Summer 1990 collection '*Hommages*', Yves Saint Laurent expressed his affection for artists, close friends, and figures who were important to him, including Marylin Monroe, Coco Chanel, Catherine Deneuve, Zizi Jeanmaire, Christian Dior, Marcel Proust and Bernard Buffet.

1992
30th anniversary of the fashion house

In 1992, the fashion house celebrated 30 years of existence at Opéra Bastille.

Universal Exposition of Seville

Yves Saint Laurent presented a catwalk show in the French pavilion at the Universal Exposition of Seville to demonstrate the excellence of French haute couture.

1993
Champagne

Yves Saint Laurent released the women's fragrance *Champagne* 'for happy, bubbly, light-hearted women who sparkle'. Within three months, it became Europe's bestselling fragrance. However, the house was forced to rename it 'Yves Saint Laurent' then 'Yvresse' in 1996 following legal proceedings initiated by the Comité interprofessionnel du vin de Champagne (Champagne producers association).

1995
La Redoute

Yves Saint Laurent's tuxedo entered the mail-order catalog La Redoute in winter 1995-1996 as the season's featured design, priced at 1,400 francs for the jacket and 700 francs for the trousers, compared to around 15,000 for the set in the SAINT LAURENT *rive gauche* boutique.

1998
Stade de France

Preceding the Football World Cup, a catwalk show featuring more than 300 of the couturier's designs was held at the Stade de France and watched by 2 billion television viewers. 'As strange as the combination might seem – 300 designs exhibited to skeptical football supporters – the show was another example of what Saint Laurent has been doing for the last 40 years: bringing together masculine and feminine, high culture and popular culture, "the clash of worlds".[29]'

PAGE LEFT
Original sketch for a long
evening ensemble including
the jacket known as 'Hommage
à ma maison'. Spring/Summer
1990 haute couture collection
'*Homages*'.

ABOVE, LEFT
Three dresses in the colours
of the French flag. Homage to
Georges Braque. Fashion show
organised for the Universal
Exposition of Seville, 1992.

ABOVE, RIGHT
Yves Saint Laurent surrounded
by his models on the 30th
anniversary of the fashion
house celebrated at the Opéra
Bastille, 3 February 1992.

OPPOSITE
Retrospective fashion show
with 300 models inaugurating
the World Cup Football final,
Stade de France, Saint-Denis,
12 July 1998.

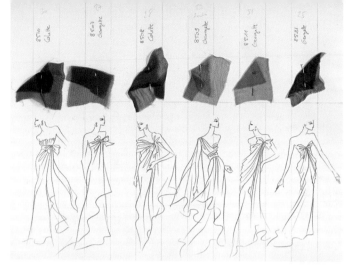

ABOVE
Collection board.
Spring/Summer 2002
haute couture collection.

OPPOSITE
Evening gown worn by Amalia
Vairelli. Spring/Summer 2002
haute couture collection.
Final retrospective fashion
show, Centre Georges-
Pompidou, Paris,
22 January 2002.

BELOW
Dialogue avec l'art, view of
the inaugural exhibition
of the Fondation Pierre Bergé –
Yves Saint Laurent, Paris, 2004.
Photograph by Luc Castel.

1999
The house changes hands

The Yves Saint Laurent Group was purchased by the Pinault-Printemps-Redoute Group (today Kering). However, the fashion house remained under the direction of Yves Saint Laurent and Pierre Bergé.

2002
Final catwalk show

On 7 January, 2002, during an emotional press conference, Yves Saint Laurent said farewell to haute couture and announced the shuttering of the fashion house. Several days later, on 22 January, he presented his final catwalk show at the Centre Georges-Pompidou as a retrospective of his 40-year career. More than 300 iconic designs were presented, as well as several creations from the final Spring/Summer 2002 collection.

Fondation Pierre Bergé – Yves Saint Laurent

Created following the fashion house's closure, the Fondation Pierre Bergé – Yves Saint Laurent, recognised as promoting the public interest, set three objectives: preserving and diffusing Yves Saint Laurent's work, and supporting cultural projects.

2004
Conversation with art

The Fondation's exhibition spaces open to the public on the premises of the former fashion house. The exhibition *'Yves Saint Laurent, dialogue avec l'art' (Yves Saint Laurent, a conversation with art)* inaugurated a long series of exhibitions focused as much on the couturier as on painting, decorative arts and photography.

2007
Legion of Honour

Yves Saint Laurent was elevated to the rank of Grand Officer of the Legion of Honour by the French President, Nicolas Sarkozy.

2008
Death

On 1 June, 2008, Yves Saint Laurent passed away in his Parisian home at the age of 71. His ashes were scattered in the garden of his Moroccan home, the Villa Oasis, and a memorial was built in the Majorelle Garden.

BELOW
Pierre Thoretton,
Yves Saint Laurent Memorial,
Majorelle Garden, Marrakech.

Evening jacket known as Hommage à ma maison (Homage to my house)

Spring/Summer 1990 haute couture collection.
Prototype. Atelier Georges.
Short organza silk jacket (Maison Abraham) embroidered
with gold metallic thread and silk thread, sequins,
crystals and strass (Maison Lesage).

Inv. HC1990E113
Photograph by Alexandre Guirkinger

'One day, Yves Saint Laurent calls François Lesage. "Come
see." He runs over. Saint Laurent shows him the reflection
of the crystal chandelier and the Paris sky in the mirror [...],
and he says, "I want that." Mr Lesage comes back with three
versions: morning light, afternoon light and evening light.
Saint Laurent cries, "It's marvellous! We'll do them all."
At the rate of 350 hours of embroidery for each piece...[30]'
In the end, a single design was completed. A true
accomplishment, it bears the poetic name Hommage
à ma maison (Homage to my house).

1990

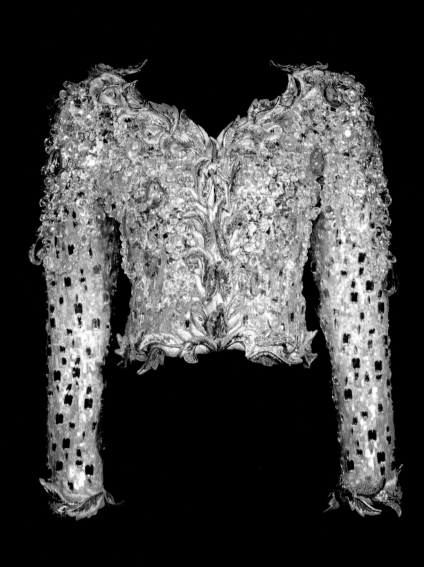

Long evening ensemble

Autumn/Winter 1990 haute couture collection.
Prototype. Atelier Jean-Pierre and Jacqueline.
Coat in pheasant and rhea feathers (Maison Lemarié),
dress in tiger-print chiffon (Maison Abraham).
Inv. HC1990H082
Photograph by Alexandre Guirkinger

Inspiration of the animal variety appears often in Yves Saint
Laurent's work: flashy rooster, ostrich and bird of paradise
feathers, and colourful fur and leather adorn many outfits.
The couturier also played with trompe-l'œil prints and
embroidery mimicking fur, crocodile leather, or snake and
fish scales, adding a touch of the wild to the ordered world
of haute couture. This evening ensemble, composed of
a coat covered in feathers, resulted from a request the
couturier made to feather worker Lemarié. 'I would like
a feathered coat that resembles a lion.' And so more
than 3,000 pheasant, vulture and rhea feathers were died
and sewn, one by one, onto very light organza.

Long evening gown

Spring/Summer 2002 haute couture collection.
Prototype. Atelier Georgette.
Silk chiffon gown (Maison Bianchini).

Inv. HC2002E031
Photograph by Alexandre Guirkinger

For his final show, Yves Saint Laurent created only several
new designs, including a series of airy chiffon dresses
that seem to hang by a thread. A defining moment of his
work, this dress is the very image of outline, beauty of colour
and chiffon's evanescence. It illustrates the garment's
perfect flowing architecture.

'When I work, first I think about paring down more
and more. Maybe there will be nothing left at the end...
I would like to achieve that level where you can say:
it's nothing and it's everything.'

2002

Behind the Scenes

More than 200 people worked enthusiastically together, with as much dedication and loyalty as an extended family, on each collection. The heart of the house was located on the first floor. There, Yves Saint Laurent worked with a team of six or seven collaborators, including Anne-Marie Muñoz, Loulou de La Falaise and several assistants, in a bright, understated space. The workshops were divided between '*flou*' (charged with creating fluid garments like dresses and blouses) and 'tailoring' (charged with creating more structured pieces like suits and tuxedos), in addition to a 'hat' workshop and a 'shoe' workshop. Dressing rooms for models, as well as warehousing, packaging, sales, press and administration comprised this feverishly paced 'hive'.

The Creative Process

From first sketch to final product, the collection creation process included a series of steps that were carried out over the month and a half before presentation. The year was organised around two haute couture collections: the Spring/Summer collection presented in January, and the Autumn/Winter collection presented in July.

Collections generally began in Morocco to where Yves Saint Laurent withdrew the first two weeks of each December and June. Paper and a Staedtler 2B pencil sufficed to design the collection in record time. He produced several hundred drawings in a few days.

Back in Paris, the couturier and Anne-Marie Muñoz, the studio director, gathered the *premiers d'atelier,* or workshop managers, all impatient to discover the new collection. Out of hundreds of sketches, some would be selected, others not. Sketches that were not retained were achieved as 'research sketches'. Each manager left the meeting with treasures to unlock.

Several weeks before the catwalk show, design creation began with toile creation. Fabric used in haute couture is very expensive; no one risked cutting it before every last detail had been decided upon on the toile, like a mock up in white cotton. In each workshop, the drawing took on three dimensions: first worked on a dressmakers form, the toile was mounted and adjusted, until it communicated the couturier's initial intention. The toiles were then presented to Yves Saint Laurent on a 'house model'. These young women worked for the house – hired for fashion fittings – and were called to the workshops and studio. Some of them were chosen to walk the podium during the haute couture show. The human mannequin was indispensable for evaluating how a garment moved.

In the bright studio, the toiles were studied one by one, by Yves Saint Laurent's keen eye, in the reflection of the large mirror. If he liked the design, he validated it; if not, the design was reworked and a second viewing was organised. Sometimes designs were abandoned.

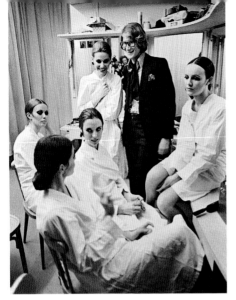

ABOVE
Yves Saint Laurent surrounded
by his models from the Spring/
Summer 1969 haute couture
collection, fitting rooms at 30 bis
Rue Spontini, Paris, January 1969.
OPPOSITE
Yves Saint Laurent and Gustav
Zumsteg, from Maison Abraham,
choosing fabrics for a collection,
studio at 30 bis Rue Spontini,
Paris, 1971.

Once the toile was approved, fabrics were chosen from a selection ordered well ahead of time. Different criteria were taken into consideration during the selection process: weight, drape, colour, pattern, etc. Details like embroidery, buttons, or other embellishments were decided upon at this stage. As they went along, information about the garment was recorded on atelier specification sheets called 'Bibles'; these identity documents contained details about suppliers, accessories, fabrics and more.

The toile was then disassembled by the workshop director in order to create the pattern, used to cut the design from the final fabrics. The pieces were then assembled, 'mounted', by a skilled *première main*, assisted by a *seconde main*. Then, the design was presented to Yves Saint Laurent for one or two fittings, until it was considered perfect. Another document, called a handling or production form, stated the fabric, the quantity used, and the number of hours necessary to create the design. This information was used to calculate the price of the garment.

The final design was delivered several days, or even several hours, before the show, at which point it had to be accessorised. In the back rooms, Loulou de La Falaise and her team suggested hats, gloves, shoes and jewellery, created, for the most part, by external suppliers according to the collection theme.

Designs were recorded by typology ('Suits', 'Short Evening', 'Long Evening', 'Tuxedos') on collection boards that gave the couturier an overview of the entire collection and made it possible to determine before the show the order in which the designs would be presented.

Invitation cards were sent to clients, buyers, journalists and friends. The day of the show, the name of each guest, as well as a collection programme, with a presentation and description of each design, were placed on chairs arranged around the podium. Initially presented plainly in the fashion house in silence, with designs announced in order by the 'voice' (a person situated at the front of the podium), from 1976 on, collections were presented in the ballroom at the Inter-Continental Hotel, to music, with a taste for dramatisation and the spectacular.

The very next day, clients were welcomed in the fashion house's reception rooms where they ordered their selected designs from an assigned saleswoman, who followed the two or three fittings necessary with the workshop manager before final delivery of the custom garment. For the most loyal clients, a dressmakers model was even created according to their measurements.

OPPOSITE AND BELOW
Yves Saint Laurent during
a collection preparation,
studio at 5 Avenue Marceau,
Paris, 1986.

From Fashion House to Museum

'Do you think posterity is important?
— Yes, I would like my dresses and my drawings to be studied in a hundred years.'
(Yves Saint Laurent, 1992)

To date, the museum's collections, property of the Fondation Pierre Bergé –
Yves Saint Laurent, are unequalled in the international world of haute couture.
A true pioneer, Yves Saint Laurent is the only designer of his generation to have
systematically archived his work since the fashion house was first created.
The heritage preserved by the Fondation is a unique treasure that shows the
creation and lives of garments. It is also possible to reconstruct a garment's entire
creative process and to situate it within its historical context for visitors.

    The creation of two Yves Saint Laurent museums, one in Paris and one in
Marrakech, is the result of the couturier's pioneering effort and a long process
of making his work part of cultural heritage.

    In 1964, Yves Saint Laurent began keeping a selection of prototypes from
each of his collections. The prototype is the design created by the couturier,
produced by the workshops under his supervision, and presented at the catwalk
show. It differs from client garments created in the weeks following the show
according to their specific measurements and desires. Some prototypes are
conserved with their accessories (jewellery, shoes, gloves, hats, etc.).
The totality of sketches and documents surrounding the creative process
for each collection is also carefully archived; the same is true for photographs,
newspaper and magazine articles, and objects that relate to the life of the
fashion house.

    In 1981, Hector Pascual, theatre designer and costume maker, whom
Yves Saint Laurent met through Roland Petit, took over the archives. In 1982,
the notation 'M' then 'Museum', appeared on workshops sheets next to each
piece chosen by Yves Saint Laurent. The conservation process began to take a
systematic approach and the selected garments were removed from distribution.

    The year 1983 marked a shift, with the couturier entering the Metropolitan
Museum of Art in New York at the invitation of Diana Vreeland, former editor-
in-chief of *Harper's Bazaar* and *Vogue,* then consultant for the museum's Costume
Institute, making him the first fashion designer to be exhibited in a museum
during his lifetime.

    In 1997, a new page was turned with the creation of the Association pour le
rayonnement de l'œuvre d'Yves Saint Laurent (Association for the Celebration
of Yves Saint Laurent's Legacy), with premises at La Villette. Conservation areas
worthy of a museum were set up to store garments under ideal conditions.
A resource space was made available to students and researchers, and an
exhibition space opened to the public.

On 7 January, 2002, Yves Saint Laurent announced at a press conference that his career had come to an end. The fashion house became the Fondation Pierre Bergé – Yves Saint Laurent. Recognised as promoting the public interest on 5 December, 2002, it opened on the premises of the former fashion house on 10 March, 2004, following major renovation.

The Fondation's primary mission is to guarantee the conservation and diffusion of Yves Saint Laurent's work. Museum-quality stockrooms have been installed where workshops once stood. The former reception rooms for haute couture clients have been transformed into exhibition spaces where, starting in 2004, fashion, painting, photography and decorative art exhibitions are held, always in connection with the world of Yves Saint Laurent and Pierre Bergé.

The year 2017 was a landmark year in the in the process of making YSL's legacy available to the public with the creation of two museums dedicated to the couturier, one in Paris, in the historic fashion house, and the other in Marrakech, a stone's throw from the Majorelle Garden. A change in status accompanied this landmark: the Yves Saint Laurent Paris Museum, charged with collection conservation, received the designation 'museum of France'. The works are henceforth protected by virtue of their inalienability and imprescriptibility, both fundamental principles of museum law.

Conscious of the need to preserve the work of a creator and a fashion house, Pierre Bergé and Yves Saint Laurent, early on and before anyone else, took a systematic approach to the preservation of creations. The Yves Saint Laurent Paris Museum was declared a pioneering museum by virtue of its former mission, which it continued, as much as for the new one it invented.

The Museum's Hidden Treasures

The museum's holdings include a variety of objects related to the life and work of Yves Saint Laurent and his fashion house. The treasures conserved by Pierre Bergé and Yves Saint Laurent are preserved according to museum standards, in Compactus® (modular, mobile shelving) under controlled climatic conditions (18 degrees Celsius, 50-55% humidity). A conservation team has been assembled over the years with the principle missions to preserve, study, inventory, enrich and showcase the collections.

Graphic arts

More than 20,000 works related to haute couture design creation make up the graphic arts collection. The museum holds a total of 8,500 original sketches, 9,500 'Bibles', and 1,300 collection boards, in addition to 2,600 costume and set design sketches for theatre, ballet, cinema, music-hall and other events.

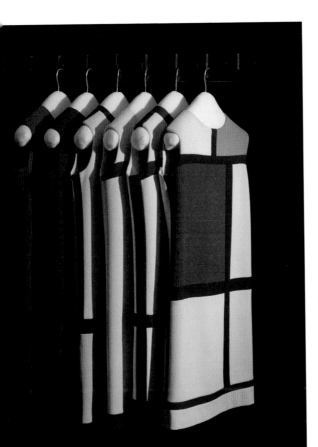

OPPOSITE
Six cocktail dresses.
From left to right: two dresses
in homage to Serge Poliakoff
and four dresses in homage
to Piet Mondrian.
Autumn/Winter 1965
haute couture collection.
Photograph by Sophie Carre.

ABOVE
Accessories archives at the Yves Saint Laurent Paris Museum,
5 Avenue Marceau, Paris, 2012. Photograph by Luc Castel.

Textiles

To date, the museum collection includes more than 7,000 haute couture designs. The core holdings are regularly enriched with acquisitions and donations. The holdings include the totality of haute couture collections presented by Yves Saint Laurent between 1962 and 2002. Several hundred outfits from SAINT LAURENT *rive gauche* ready-to-wear collections are also conserved, as well as certain stage costumes.

Accessories

The 8,500 haute couture accessories were collected at the same time as the clothing, and include jewellery, scarves, hats, headdresses, gloves, shoes, bags and flowers that enable looks to be recreated in their entirety.

Art Photographs

More than 1,000 photographs by the most prestigious photographers of the 20th century – Irving Penn, Richard Avedon, Helmut Newton, David Seidner, Arthur Elgort, Jeanloup Sieff and Marc Riboud – are safely conserved.

Documentary holdings

The documentary holdings include garment mock ups, patterns, client mannequins, samples, trays of buttons, wood and plaiting materials (hat blocks), handling forms, sales record books (by design or by client), documentation, personal photographs and photographs of catwalk shows, as well as sound and audiovisual archives. The couturier's correspondence and his personal library also enrich this priceless collection.

Miscellaneous works

The museum conserves works from the couturier's childhood, like the 11 'Paper Dolls' and their wardrobes, several paintings and illustrated books. Also included are works he created in addition to his haute couture creations, like the 36 'LOVE' greeting cards and their preparatory sketches in poster format, and the forty-some original boards for the comic book *La Vilaine Lulu* created in 1956.

Paintings

The museum owns famous portraits of the couturier, like the one created by Bernard Buffet in 1958 and those painted by Andy Warhol in 1972.

Endnotes

1. *Yves Saint Laurent: 25 Years of Design*, New York, Metropolitan Museum of Art, 14 December 1983 – 2 September 1984, New York, Clarkson N. Potter, Inc., 1983, p. 15.

2. Eugenia Sheppard, *Herald Tribune*, 31 January, 1958.

3. 'Yves Saint Laurent le nouvel enfant triste' in *L'Express*, 6 February 1958.

4. *Yves Saint Laurent: 25 Years of Design*, *op. cit.*, p. 20.

5. Handwritten note by Yves Saint Laurent, s. d., Yves Saint Laurent Museum Paris.

6. Claude Berthod, interview with Yves Saint Laurent, Dim Dam Dom, 10 March 1968.

7. Patrick Thévenon, 'Le couturier qui a pensé aux femmes d'aujourd'hui', *Candide*, 15 August 1965.

8. Collective work, *Yves Saint Laurent - Forty Years of Creation 1958-1998*, New York, International Festival of Fashion Photography, 1998, p. 112

9. Patrick Thévenon, 'Le couturier qui a pensé aux femmes d'aujourd'hui', *Candide*, 15 August 1965.

10. Quoted in Laurence Benaïm, *Yves Saint Laurent*, Paris, Grasset, 2002.

11. Handwritten note by Yves Saint Laurent, s. d., Yves Saint Laurent Museum Paris.

12. 'Africa: Saint Laurent', *Harper's Bazaar* (United States), 1 March 1967.

13. Handwritten note by Yves Saint Laurent, s. d., Yves Saint Laurent Museum Paris.

14. 'Le 7ᵉ Festival International de la photo de mode s'ouvre sur les 40 ans d'Yves Saint Laurent', *Photo* (France), 1 April 1998.

15. *Les Lettres françaises*, 8 March 1972.

16. André Léon Tallet, 'YSL on Opium', *Women's Wear Daily*, 18 September 1978.

17. *Elle* (France), 1 mars 1971.

18. Fiona Levis, *Yves Saint Laurent, l'homme couleur de temps*, Paris, Éditions du Rocher, 2008, p. 132.

19. Gonzague Saint Bris, 'Yves Saint Laurent ou l'honneur de souffrir', *Femme* (France), 1 March 1992.

20. Marcel Proust, *À la recherche du temps perdu. Le côté de Guermantes*, Paris, Gallimard, 1920-1921.

21. 'Yves Saint Laurent ou le regard du peintre', *Vogue* (Paris), 1 September 1976.

22. Handwritten note by Yves Saint Laurent, s. d., Yves Saint Laurent Museum Paris.

23. Handwritten note by Yves Saint Laurent, s. d., Yves Saint Laurent Museum Paris.

24. http://museeyourcenar.chez.com/l_academie_francaise_034.htm

25. Handwritten note by Yves Saint Laurent, 1983, Yves Saint Laurent Paris Museum.

26. *Yves Saint Laurent. Dialogue avec l'art*, Paris, Fondation Pierre Bergé – Yves Saint Laurent, 10 March – 31 October 2004, preface by Dominique Païni, Paris, Fondation Pierre Bergé – Yves Saint Laurent, 2004, p. 9.

27. Interview with Pierre Bergé at AFP on the occasion of the exhibition 'Une passion marocaine ', Fondation Pierre Bergé – Yves Saint Laurent, (14 March – 31 August 2008).

28. Yves Saint Laurent's farewell speech to haute couture, 7 January 2002, 5 avenue Marceau, Paris.

29. Pierre Bergé, 12 July 1998 in *Time Magazine*.

30. *L'Officiel de la mode*, March 1990.

Copyrights and photo credits

The textiles, accessories, sketches and personal documents reproduced in this book are held in the Yves Saint Laurent Paris Museum, as are a majority of the photographs.

Yves Saint Laurent Paris Museum

Director
Olivier Flaviano

Heritage manager, collection director
Aurélie Samuel

Text, picture research and
editorial coordination
Lola Fournier
Deputy director of collections

With the participation of the Conservation team:
**Alice Coulon-Saillard, Domitille Éblé,
Laurence Neveu and Leslie Veyrat**

Réunion des musées nationaux – Grand Palais

Publishing Director
Sophie Laporte

Head of publications
Muriel Rausch

Editorial Coordinator
Elsa Belaieff

Graphic Design
Bernard Lagacé and Agnès Rousseaux

Translation
Kate Robinson

Correction
Claire Liron-Patterson

Production Manager
Isabelle Loric

Photoengraving
Apex Graphic, Paris

Printed on Arctic Volume White 130 g/m² paper,
www.arcticpaper.com, in August 2019
by Ingoprint, Barcelone, Espagne.

First Legal Deposit
September 2017

Legal Deposit
August 2019

ISBN 978-2-7118-7057-8
GK 397057

INSIDE BACK COVER
Acrostic poem handwritten
by Yves Saint Laurent.

Y for Yves
V for Victory
E for Energy
S for Smile

S for Sun
A for Adoration
I for Immense
N for Necessary
T for Timeless

L for Laurent
A for Aurora
U for Unique
R for Renaissance
E for Eternity
N for Night
T for Tenderness